THE COMPLETE GUIDE TO BUILDING YOUR BRAND WITH SNAPCHAT

MATT MIZELL

No time to figure it all out?

Hire Matt to help build your
brand or generate buzz for your event by
visiting www.mattmizell.com/snapmatt.

Download the digital version of this book for FREE
at www.mattmizell.com/free-snapchat-book.

Dedicated to those who invest more
in people than the bottom line.

"Marketing is no longer about the stuff that you make, but about the stories you tell."
— SETH GODIN

CONTENTS ► *Indicates video tutorial*

HOW TO USE THIS GUIDE

This guide will walk you through exactly how to generate excitement and buzz for your brand, organization, company, band, church, team, group, program or event by using Snapchat in an upcoming advertising campaign. *(For simplicity, the terms "brand" and "event" will primarily be used throughout this guide from here forward.)*

If you are new to using the Snapchat app, be sure to read the chapter entitled *How to Navigate the Snapchat App* to get an overview of the app and get better acquainted with its functionality. You may also watch the video tutorial for the chapter to see exactly what the app looks like on a real device.

Speaking of videos, each chapter that has a video included provides two ways to access the video:

1) The URL to the video is available for you to manually type into your computer, or
2) You may use your mobile device to scan the barcode that looks like this:

Most smartphones have the capability to scan QR codes by using nearly any barcode reader app. QR codes can be read by using your Snapchat app.

To scan a QR code, open up Snapchat on your mobile device, point the camera at the code, and tap and hold your screen for a few seconds for Snapchat to read the QR code. Within 2-3 seconds, you should be prompted within Snapchat to open the URL in your internet browser.

If you do not have Snapchat installed on your mobile device, you may opt for another free app such as QR Code Reader. The QR Code Reader app is available on iOS and Android and can be downloaded at www.scan.me. If you don't already have a QR code or barcode reader on your device, take a minute to download Snapchat or another QR code reader right now.

If you already have somewhat of a working knowledge of Snapchat, don't feel as though you have to read every page of this guide or follow it in order. Use the chapter titles in the Contents and flip directly to what you would like to learn.

Given the nature of technology, there is a possibility that

some of the instructions in this guide have become outdated by the time you read this. If you happen to find something that no longer works or is no longer available, please send me an email at matt@mattmizell.com so I can make any revisions necessary for future editions of this book.

Now that you hopefully have Snapchat or another QR code reader installed, let's get started!

WHY SNAPCHAT ISN'T AS SHADY AS IT ONCE WAS

In September of 2016, Snapchat discreetly announced they changed their company name to Snap, Inc.

This subtle name change comes as a result of the Snapchat brand gaining more traction as a popular household name in the last few years.

In addition, they are adding a physical product to their portfolio called Spectacles, which are glasses that will likely compete with GoPro. Considering the Snapchat website claims they are primarily a camera company, it makes sense why they would shorten their name to Snap.

While the company name has been changed to Snap, Snapchat still exists as one of Snap's brands as an app.

The fact that the Snapchat app has gone so mainstream is pretty impressive considering its rough start with such a poor reputation among adults.

Its bad reputation was a result of the app's enticement for kids to exchange inappropriate pictures with one another since images disappear after a few seconds.

In fact, I was adamantly opposed to parents allowing their kids to use Snapchat, and even made a video in 2013 encouraging parents to ban the app from their kids' devices.

However, even I have jumped on board and I now utilize Snap more than any other social media platform. It's not that I have changed my morals or values. Rather, Snapchat changed the way users can interact with the app. In other words, Snapchat has grown up a bit.

There are 4 reasons why I now use Snapchat on a consistent basis:

1. **Improved transparency**

Snapchat used to not allow users to take screenshots of pictures. This encouraged teenagers to send scandalous pics to each other since images disappeared after a few seconds.

However, kids still found a way to capture images before they disappeared, so Snap eventually just built in the feature so now it's part of the app.

Not only did Snap add the ability to screenshot images, but the app now tells you *who* took a screenshot of *what* image.

By building the screenshot capability directly into the app, teenagers now realize that no photo is guaranteed to disappear, so they have wisely become more cautious about what types of images they post both privately and publicly.

With the improved transparency, Snapchat has gained notoriety and has wiped away much of its bad reputation.

2. Snapchat has gone mainstream

Most major news outlets and dozens of brands now use Snap, and it reaches far more young people in my sphere of influence than Facebook and is on par with Instagram.

3. Snapchat reaches a massive number of youth

According to Snap, over 158 million people who use the app on a daily basis!

Of those 158 million users, over 94 million of them create Snaps every day, creating over 2.5 billion Snaps and viewing over 10 billion videos every 24 hours.

The average Snapchatter visits Snapchat more than 18 times per day with an average of 25-30 minutes of daily use.

There are reports claiming that Facebook still has quite a large following of teenagers, but in my sphere of influence,

Facebook is already dead among teens. Snapchat is rapidly becoming just as popular—if not more popular—than Instagram.

4. Cheap advertising

Most media outlets sell advertising based on CPM (cost per 1000 impressions) or CPC (cost per click). However, Snap uses neither when advertising with their geofilters.

A filter is an overlay that a user can place over their own picture, such as the name of a city or an event. While some filters are available nationwide, others are available based on geolocation.

Using a geofilter, an advertiser can create a marketing campaign that is targeted for a specific time and location, and the impressions are unlimited.

For example, if you buy $5 worth of ads on Facebook, you might reach your marketing budget for the day after 1000 people see your ad in a CPM campaign.

With Snap, if you spend $5, you could potentially have 100 uses in a 3-hour period and make 10,000 impressions. While that example shows a campaign that is 10x more effective, I have actually conducted Snap campaigns that had an ROI of 50x greater than Facebook.

If you want to run a CPC campaign where users are able to click on a button or call to action, Snap currently only offers such capability to larger national brands that they handpick.

However, if you want to generate buzz or create brand recognition at a specific geotargeted location like a CPM campaign, the ROI with Snapchat can be much higher.

Not only have I jumped onto the Snapchat bandwagon because of these 4 reasons, but with their fresh branding and new Spectacles, I believe the platform will explode with even more popularity in the next 12 months.

That is, until too many parents and businesses create their own accounts and the teens don't think it's cool anymore.

TIPS, TRICKS & HOW TO NAVIGATE SNAPCHAT ▶

Getting around the Snapchat app can be intimidating for the first time. However, once you understand the basic layout, it becomes very user-friendly.

When you open the app, it will bring you directly to the native camera so you can take a picture or video. After all, Snap is primarily a camera company, so it makes sense that the app would open directly to the camera.

Snapchat makes it easy to send and receive pictures that disappear from your device after a few seconds. While some people

a) **Where to take a picture**

When you open the app, Snapchat will by default open up the camera screen where you can take a picture.

b) **Where to take a video**

There is no toggle between still-frame photos or videos. To take a video, you simply hold the camera button down and a video will begin to record. A red line that rotates around the camera button indicates that you are recording a video.

c) **Where to add a filter**

Once you have taken a picture or video, hold down on the screen and swipe left. This will bring up a variety of color-enhancing filters as well as any geofilters that might be available. (For more on the various types of filters, read the chapter *An Introduction to Snapchat Filters*.) Once you have selected a filter, you may add more than one filter using the same process.

d) **How to add text to a photo or video**

Once you have taken a photo or video, in the upper right of the screen you will see a text icon. Tap the icon, and you will be able to write text using your keypad or using your finger as the pencil. You may change the color as you like.

e) **How to add a sticker to your photo or video**

Stickers are digital pictures you can overlay on top of your photo or video. Once you have taken a photo or video, in the upper right of the screen you will see a sticker icon. Tap the icon, and you will be able to select whatever digital sticker you wish. You can apply more than one sticker if you want. To adjust the size of the sticker, use two fingers to expand the size of the sticker larger or smaller.

f) **How to add a filter or geofilter to a pic or video**

To add a filter or geofilter, take a picture or video with Snapchat, and then swipe to the left to view a filter. Continue swiping left to view more filters.

To add multiple filters, stay on one filter you like, hold one finger on the screen while you continue swiping left with another finger. You may add up to 3 filters to a single image or video.

g) **How to add a lense to a video or picture**

To add a lense, focus the camera on a face and tap the screen once. Snapchat will open up an array of possible lenses you can apply either to a video you can record or to a still frame photo.

Some lenses will give you the ability to play games with your Snapchat camera, whereas other lenses turn your face into a puzzle that only you can solve.

h) **How to undo edits**

If you apply a filter, add text, draw on, or add a sticker

that you don't like on your picture or video, in the upper right side of the screen is a back arrow where you can undo your last action.

i) How to add friends

From the camera screen, swipe down and click the option to "Add Friends". You can add friends by username, people in your device's contact list, by Snapcode, by sharing your username, and those who are nearby.

j) How to search

You can use the search function to find friends, a group that you're in, Quick Chats, and more. When you tap the search magnifying glass icon on the top of the screen within Snapchat, you will also be given suggestions for what you might be looking for, such as friends you chat with often, groups, Publisher Stories, and recently added friends.

k) How to use Shazam within Snapchat

You can find out what song is playing without leaving the Snapchat app. Whenever you hear a song you want to know, simply tap and hold the camera screen, and Snapchat will use Shazam to find out whatever song is playing and will display it on the screen for you.

l) How to zoom with one finger

Everyone knows how to pinch to zoom on mobile devices. Snapchat now features the ability to zoom with one finger, giving you the ability to zoom while shooting video clips holding your device with one hand. To zoom with one finger, tap and hold the record button and swipe vertically up the screen while still touching the screen.

m) How to rotate your camera with one finger

Sometimes you want a selfie and sometimes you want to take a picture of what's in front of you. To easily switch back and forth from your front-facing camera to your back camera, simply double-tap your screen.

n) How to use a Snapcode

There are two ways to add a friend using a Snapcode.

    a. Open Snapchat on your mobile device, go to the camera, and tap and hold the screen while pointing your camera at a Snapcode. Your device should recognize the Snapcode and add your new friend.

    b. The second way to add a new friend with a

Snapcode is to take a picture of their Snapcode, go to "Add Friends" in Snapchat, and select the pic you took of their Snapcode.

Feel free to try it out either method by adding me as a friend using my personal Snapcode below. (Note: This book includes both Snapcodes and QR codes. Snapcodes include the Snapchat Ghost Logo in the center and have rounded corners, such as the image on this page. QR codes are squares and do not include the Snapchat Ghost Logo. You may use the Snapchat app to scan either Snapcodes or QR codes.

o) **How to send a direct message**

From the camera screen, swipe left. You will see conversations you have had with contacts. On the upper right, you will see a conversation chat icon with a plus sign. Tap that and select a contact and send them a message.

p) How to send a group message

While you are capable of sending single messages to however many friends you wish at once, those friends cannot see who else has also received your message. In a group, however, up to 16 Snapchatters can share messages that are all visible to one another. Chats sent to a group are deleted after 24 hours. To create a new group, swipe left from the camera screen and click the small chat icon with the plus sign in the upper right hand side of the chat screen.

q) How to send a pic or vid from your camera roll

From the camera screen, swipe up to reveal previous snaps. There is also a toggle to view your camera roll. Click the camera roll and select the photo you would like to send.

r) How to view someone's "story"

Seth Godin's quote at the beginning of this book mentions how marketing is now storytelling. As it relates to Snapchat, your goal is to get your brand or geofilter into people's stories. A Snapchat story is the culmination of someone's snaps (pictures and videos) within a 24-hour period. To view your own story, swipe right from the camera screen. This will display usernames of other friends you know who also have stories available to view. You may tap any of their names to start their story. Their story will consist of each of their snaps, in the order in which they were taken. You may also view your own story from the same location.

s) How to see who has viewed your story

From the story screen, tap your own story at the very top of the page. You will be able to see who has seen each of your Snaps, as well as anyone who has taken a screenshot of any of your Snaps.

t) How to view news updates

Snapchat has partnered with various news and entertainment outlets to provide interactive articles and news updates. To access news updates, swipe right on the story page after swiping right from the camera.

u) How to unlock Snapchat's special edition

Head to www.snapchat.com/ads, scroll to the bottom of the page, open the camera on your Snapchat app, and scan the Snapcode with the Snapchat winking Ghost Logo. You will open up a secret special edition news page published by Snapchat that includes all the latest and greatest updates and features as well as any cool new advertising opportunities.

v) **Where to get more tips and training**

Snap frequently posts tips and training on their own website for how to use Snapchat. Their training section is buried on their website under the "Inquiries" link at the bottom of their homepage.

Some features that are unrelated to building a brand have not been included in this publication, such as the meaning behind friend emojis, sending snaps via text, sending money to friends with Snapcash, and several others.

To read more about Snapchat features not published in this book or that have been recently added, visit https://support.snapchat.com/en-US.

Scan to view a video tutorial on this chapter, or go to:
http://mattmizell.com/how-to-navigate-the-snapchat-app

3 WAYS TO BUILD YOUR BRAND WITH SNAPCHAT

There are 3 main tools to build your brand with Snapchat:

1) **Snap Ads**
2) **Sponsored Lenses**
3) **Sponsored Geofilters**

Let's take a closer look at each option:

1) Snap Ads

Snap Ads are typically video clips that are discovered by Snapchat users that play within their mobile device. Snap Ads promote larger organizations or campaigns and build brand awareness on a national level.

Snap Ads Max Reach places ads across Our Stories, Publisher Stories, and between Snapchatters' Stories for a single day. This basically creates a 24-hour all-out Snapchat take-over for advertisers who want to get their campaign out quickly and efficiently.

Snapchat also offers Goal-Based Bidding for Snap Ads. Goal-Based Bidding allows advertisers to bid on a goal, such as impressions or swipes. Then your campaign is delivered to optimize for that goal at the lowest cost by showing your ad to Snapchatters who are most likely to take the action you want them to take. Snapchat will likely add new types of Goal-Based Bidding in the future as well.

Snapchat has also partnered with Oracle Data Cloud to provide advertisers with third-party audience segments. This gives advertisers the capability of reaching Snapchatters based on data from past purchase and buying behavior across a large number of products and sales channels.

A few companies that have successfully utilized Snap Ads include Universal, Gatorade and AT&T.

2) Sponsored Lenses

Sponsored Lenses introduce a new type of user engagement that Snap refers to as "Play Time". Play Time refers to the amount of time that a user not only views the ad, but actually interacts with it.

For example, Sponsored Lenses give the user the unique ability to wear a mask, change their look, or morph into somebody else. The possibilities are limitless for what types of lenses your organization could use to create a positive perspective for your brand. At the time of print, Sponsored Lenses are currently only available in national campaigns.

A few companies that have successfully utilized Sponsored Lenses are FOX, Michael Kors and Kraft.

3) Sponsored Geofilters

According to Snap, Sponsored Geofilters are "tiny pieces of art that always make an impression".

There are four types of Sponsored Geofilter campaigns: Event, Shared Spaces, Chain and National.

Event campaigns use geofilters that help promote an event at a specific location, such as a beauty pageant.

Shared Space campaigns use geofilters that help promote a brand in an area where multiple brands share a common area, such as an airport.

Chain campaigns use geofilters to promote specials or create brand awareness for corporations or franchises, such as Target.

National campaigns use geofilters to promote brands or events across the entire country at one time.

A few companies that have successfully utilized Sponsored Geofilters are Coca-Cola, GE and Retail Me Not. However, Sponsored Geofilters differ from Snap Ads and Sponsored Lenses because thousands of small businesses and individuals have also utilized geofilters in smaller, local campaigns to build their brands, organizations, products, services, churches, teams and more.

Large brands can benefit greatly from all three types of ads, whereas smaller brands will most likely get the most benefit by utilizing Sponsored Geofilters since they have a more targeted approach to building a brand.

If you are interested in advertising with Snap Ads or Sponsored Lenses, you may choose from a variety of Snapchat Partners who can help with targeting demographics as well as graphic design that meet Snapchat requirements. To find a Snapchat Partner, visit https://www.snapchat.com/ads/partners.

The majority of this book focuses on the utilization and implementation of Sponsored Geofilters as the primary avenue of building buzz and excitement for brands, whether they are large or small. Snapchat Partners are not necessary for launching your own custom geofilters.

AN INTRODUCTION TO ON-DEMAND GEOFILTERS

What exactly is a "geofilter"?

Before we look closer specifically at geofilters, it is important to understand that Snapchat offer two different types of filters in general:

1) Camera Filters

These filters are similar to what you will find on Instagram and Facebook. These filters change lighting and exposure and are designed to make photos look better.

2) Sponsored Geofilters

A geofilter typically includes transparent text or an image that's paid for—or sponsored—by a brand or person.

The text or image is overlaid on top of a photo someone takes within Snapchat.

It's called a geofilter because GPS coordinates determine where in the world that particular geofilter will be made available.

For example, one geofilter might be available throughout the entire country for anyone to use, whereas another geofilter might just be available in New York City, whereas another geofilter might just be available at Central Park in New York City, whereas another geofilter might just be available at a gazebo in Central Park in New York City.

Because geofilters use GPS coordinates, you can get pretty specific about where you would like a filter to be available.

While this guide will teach you how to use both types of filters, our primary focus is on geofilters.

Your creative potential is unlimited, and geofilters can be used for event promotions, marketing campaigns, weddings, sporting events, church services, and nearly anything else you can think of.

Be aware that geofilters currently do not allow someone to click on it and take them to a website, but it *does* allow you to create a call to action and allows for branding and is great for building excitement.

Geofilters are currently underutilized for advertising, yet insanely popular.

Snap refers to them as "On-Demand Geofilters" because you can purchase a geofilter and get it up and running within just a few hours.

Throughout this book, I will primarily refer to the On-Demand Geofilters simply as geofilters, but they are one in the same.

Whether you know a lot about geofilters or this is your first time discovering what they are, now is the right time to get on board since the marketplace is not yet completely flooded with them. However, that will be changing in the very near future.

WHO SHOULD USE GEOFILTERS & HOW

Anyone who organizes events, activities, or conducts business in a static location would benefit by using Snapchat geofilters.

The following pages include job titles and ideas for how to create branding and buzz by using geofilters. Of course my suggestions are not an exhaustive list, but intended to get your creative juices flowing so you can brainstorm ways that you can use geofilters for your event or organization.

Here is a list of job titles for people who could benefit from using Snapchat geofilters:

1. ENTREPRENEURS
2. MARKETERS
3. PROMOTERS
4. SOCIAL MEDIA MANAGERS
5. PUBLIC RELATION SPECIALISTS
6. PHOTOGRAPHERS
7. DIRECTORS
8. ACTORS
9. TEACHERS

10. YOUTH PASTORS

11. COACHES

12. FITNESS INSTRUCTORS

13. MODELS

14. ARTISTS

15. MUSICIANS, BANDS & DJS

16. FASHION DESIGNERS

17. INTERIOR DESIGNERS

18. ARCHITECTS

19. RESTAURANTEURS

20. CHEFS

21. FOOD TRUCKS

22. SPA OWNERS

23. MASSAGE THERAPISTS

24. MANICURISTS

25. CHIROPRACTORS

26. CONSTRUCTION LABORERS

27. FUNDRAISERS

28. REALTORS

29. BOOKSTORE OWNER

30. LIBRARIANS

31. VETERINARIANS

32. LAWYERS

33. DENTISTS

34. WAITERS/WAITRESSES

35. AUTHORS

36. POLITICIANS

37. FUNERAL DIRECTORS

38. NON-PROFITS

1. ENTREPRENEURS

There are countless ideas for Snapchat geofilters if you are an entrepreneur. The added benefit is that you likely have a pretty creative mind for how to do business, which means you probably have ideas constantly swirling within your mind about how to run your company different and better than yesterday.

If you have a physical brick-and-mortar building, consider running an annual geofilter that continuously stays active all year long.

You could also run geofilter campaigns for each new product launch, for sales, big events, promotions, repeat customers, or holidays.

If you own a franchise, make sure that corporate allows you to use your brand logo within social media campaigns. If you are free to use your company logo as you wish, you could have new and fresh geofilter campaigns on a consistent basis.

The sky is the limit for entrepreneurs since you have so many ways to incorporate geofilters to build your brand with buzz, excitement and exclusivity.

2. MARKETERS

If you work for a marketing or advertising agency, you likely have many clients that pay your company to build brand and product awareness.

Snapchat geofilters will probably not be an all-inclusive advertising campaign for your clients, but they should definitely be a part of your overall package of what you can include. You can brainstorm ways for your clients' to create buzz and excitement by incorporating geofilters into what they're already doing.

Considering Snapchat geofilters are still a relatively new form of advertising, offering them to your clients will likely separate your advertising agency from your competitors.

3. PROMOTERS

No matter what you're promoting, geofilters can help. If you are a concert promoter, geofilters are a must. By setting up a geofilter at a show or performance, you can create a simple and viral campaign that has the potential to reach tens of thousands of others.

The benefit you are working with as a promoter is that you likely already have raving fans who will gladly promote your brand for free, so when they have the opportunity, they will share your geofilter and convince others who are with them to do the same.

For promoters, using Snapchat geofilters is a must.

4. SOCIAL MEDIA MANAGERS

If you're in charge of an organization's social media account, be sure to include Snapchat as a part of your portfolio. Not only can you create a Snapchat account for your clients, but be sure to set up geofilters for any events they are hosting.

Be sure to tell people who attend those events to look for the geofilter so your clients become aware that you're using social media in cutting-edge ways.

5. PUBLIC RELATIONS SPECIALISTS

As a PR Specialist, one of your main roles is to ensure that your organization looks good to the public. Anytime you have a press release, create a geofilter that reporters or your staff can use to help generate positive buzz.

Add geofilters to events where guests are invited. Don't forget that you can add geofilters across the entire nation, so if you are responsible for a large corporation, you can help create positive buzz from thousands of miles away in a way that appears to be a grass roots type of campaign to the locals who are present.

6. PHOTOGRAPHERS

As a professional photographer, you may feel as though using Snapchat will take away from the professionalism of your brand. You couldn't more wrong.

Using geofilters at events, school dances, photo shoots, weddings, and anywhere else you shoot, you create incredible brand awareness for your services.

At any given time, there are hundreds of cameras roaming around any event at which you're shooting.

While photos from those cameras will soon flood the internet and social media, what they probably lack is your quality and creativity.

The faster you can upload your quality images from your event, the faster you will build your brand. If your photos are among the first to show up online, they will quickly become THE photos that are tagged and shared.

Therefore, as a photographer, you have a unique advantage over other people who also want to use geofilters, because yours have a greater likelihood of going viral naturally.

In addition to your quality pics having a great chance to go viral, you also become the brand that is known and used by the army of other photographers that are also at the event.

By making a generic event geofilter that includes your logo at the bottom, you are essentially enlisting a sea of people to help you spread your brand.

If you want to differentiate the pictures you have taken verses those who have simply used your geofilter, create a separate geofilter: one for the guests, and one for your exclusive use.

To learn how to offer geofilters for your guests and separate geofilters that are exclusive to just you, read the chapter toward the end of this book entitled *How to Take the "Geo" Out of the Filter.*

Another idea to consider is to have an assistant photographer who goes along with you on a shoot to create the behind-the-scenes pics to post online. This way, there is no expectation that your images have to be edited since they will have the more raw feel to them.

You have many avenues to use geofilters as a professional photographer, so get creative and use this as a tool to separate your brand from all the rest.

Remember that others can screenshot and share your images from their own accounts, so the better you make your pictures, the greater reach you will have.

7. DIRECTORS

As a director of any group or organization, you are likely responsible for helping produce events throughout the year.

Because these events are likely planned well in advance, you have the ability to meet with your staff and brainstorm ideas for geofilters well before you need to use them.

For tips on maximizing your geofilter campaigns, be sure to read the chapter entitled *Where You Should Be Getting Creative Advice*.

8. ACTORS

Get creative for your next shoot or play by including a geofilter at your next performance. By flooding Snapchat stories with your acting video clips, you never know who you will reach. If you have multiple performances, create your geofilter for the first performance so it informs others that they can come see you perform.

Your geofilter can't include a real picture of you, but you can get a caricature made of you based on a real photo, and you can use your caricature in your geofilter.

Your fans will be taking pictures right alongside your caricature as if they're standing next to you. For an example of a caricature geofilter, check out the next chapter entitled *Samples Geofilters.*

9. TEACHERS

For special projects and assignments, use geofilters to engage where students already are.

You can also convince your principal to let you set up a geofilter for assemblies, competitions or graduation ceremonies.

10. YOUTH PASTORS

Since most youth pastors put on all sorts of events, you can create geofilters for every unique event as well as static geofilter for every regular service time you offer.

In addition, you can set up special campaigns using puzzles, school battles, and birthday celebrations. For more information on creative ways to use geofilters, see chapters entitled *How to Design Geofilter Puzzles, How to Create a Geofilter Battle,* and *Celebrating Special Events with Geofilters.*

11. COACHES

Geofilters give you an incredible way to build team unity. Set up a geofilter wherever your practices or games are, and encourage your team players to use the geofilters with one another. In addition to getting your team in the social media spotlight, your geofilters will give players the reason to join together for their own photo shoots.

If you want to emphasize camaraderie, create a geofilter during a game that shows both teams' logos instead of just your own. That way the other team's players and fans can use the geofilter as well, and you will be serving them and not just competing against them.

Another option is to set up a geofilter for your team's win timed for when your game or competition is scheduled to conclude. You might lose the game, in which case you simply don't tell anyone about the existence of your geofilter. If, however, you win, begin telling your players that a Snapchat filter is set up for the win, and they will spread it like wildfire!

12. <u>FITNESS INSTRUCTORS</u>

Set up geofilters at your gym so those who are working out can upload pics as they work out. As they are proud of their progress, they will naturally want to share their results. Having your gym name or your own personal brand associated with the personal progress and goals of those who are working out, you will generate much more awareness for the service you offer. The best part is— your brand will likely be associated with positive results since that is what people want to share most.

13. MODELS

If you are a model, set up a geofilter on location where you are having a photo shoot. Have a friend take behind-the-scenes pics using a geofilter. Just be sure to get permission from the brand who has hired you to make sure they're okay with you taking personal photos before their official photos are released.

14. ARTISTS

As an artist, you can set up a custom geofilter at your gallery showing. While most galleries forbid taking pictures, you can encourage it with the use of your own geofilter. This way your brand name is associated with all of your artwork, and people will be more likely to search for your name online.

If you're worried about copyright infringement, you probably shouldn't be considering the images uploaded to Snapchat won't be high resolution for reprinting. Even if someone did take an image without a filter, the added benefit from Snapchat geofilter exposure would likely outweigh any lost revenue from someone attempting to reprint your images. Of course, use your own discretion and make your own decision about your risk verses reward.

15. MUSICIANS, BANDS & DJS

Geofilters are an easy win for musicians, bands and DJs! Because geofilters also allow the use of videos and not just pictures, guests at your shows can upload video clips with your geofilter as an overlay. This will help spread your music with your actual logo rather than uploaded clips that have no branding attached to them. Consider using geofilters for each concert, show, and gig, as well as studio sessions where other producers and guests may use your geofilter as well.

You could even create a custom geofilter exclusively for backstage or VIP guests by pinpointing your GPS coordinates.

For instructions on how to create geofences for specific locations, read the chapter entitled *How to Set Up a Filter's Geofence.*

16. FASHION DESIGNERS

Roll out the design process of some your upcoming line by using custom geofilters. If you ever have a fashion show, geofilters are a must! It's an easy way for fans to connect with your brand, and it sets you up as an authoritative brand among a sea of other competing brands.

17. INTERIOR DECORATORS

Create a custom geofilter at your store or next showcase. As people take pictures of your creations, designs and ideas, they can share them with your branding, building a stronger connection between your style and your brand's identity. This helps your style become more recognizable to the outside world who may not yet be familiar with your work.

18. ARCHITECTS

After a construction project is complete, set up a geofilter over your new building, allowing anyone who visits the building to take a picture with the branding of your firm that created it. Think of creative ways to engage visitors rather than using a stale geofilter, but if you have fun with it, you will begin to establish a connection to a new type of customer since you will be interacting with visitors to your building rather than just the construction company that is following your orders.

For tips on making sure your geofilter isn't boring, read the chapter entitled *How to Ensure Your Geofilter Isn't Lame.*

19. RESTAURANTEURS

Whether you offer fast food or fine dining, a Snapchat geofilter is a must for restaurants! It's too easy of a win to neglect this opportunity.

If you offer fast food, you will have clients who may be coming in with friends to grab a quick bite as they head to or from other events. Your geofilter is a milestone along their way for their day's journey.

If you offer fine dining, your customers will want to show off the food they order and how its presented. You could even have your waiters/waitresses ask customers if they have Snapchat, and offer to take a branded picture for customers using your filter for them.

Regardless of the type of food you serve, restaurateurs have one of the biggest advantages when it comes to using geofilters.

20. CHEFS

As a chef, many of your customers will want to take a photo of their food the moment it comes out. Get extra exposure out of that moment while building your Snapchat following at the same time.

Include a Snapcode on your menu so customers can add you as a friend, giving you the chance to connect with them in the future with specials, new menu items, behind-the-scenes kitchen tours, etc.

21. FOOD TRUCKS

Food truck operators can create serious buzz using geofilters. If you know what locations you will be visiting prior to your arrival, set up geofilters in each location during the time frames you expect to be there.

If your truck is one of many that are available at a location or event, you could include a 10% off discount on the geofilter design to encourage other people to come use it while you're at the same location. As your geofilter is used, it also becomes an ongoing marketing campaign to encourage immediate use. Friends of those who post will likely be those who use your discount geofilter since they have an exclusive deal that nobody else gets.

Put a picture of your Snapcode on the outside of your truck so Snapchat users know that you're on Snapchat. Include a message beneath your Snapcode that says "Look for our geofilter!" and you'll be on your way to generating fun and exciting buzz.

Your customers will likely post pics with your food and your truck along with their friends.

To see an example of a Snapcode, read the chapter entitled *How to Navigate the Snapchat App*.

22. <u>SPA OWNERS</u>

Set up a geofilter at your spa so your customers can share pictures of the serene and relaxing environment.

Unlike other business owners, however, you might not promote your geofilter so you're not encouraging customers to be on their devices when they should be focused on relaxing and disconnecting.

Users who do find your geofilter, however, will feel that it is a pleasant and unexpected surprise. Therefore, consider adding a 10% discount to your store within your geofilter since most Snapchat customers will feel they have discovered an exclusive hidden offer that most people never find.

23. MASSAGE THERAPISTS

Capture excitement as customers wait before their massage and capture the relaxed state of mind at the end of their massage by offering custom geofilters. While some people may not want to take pictures after their massage is over, you could give incentives if they do, such as a transferrable coupon for 15% off a future visit in exchange for them using your geofilter.

24. MANICURISTS

Create a custom business card that includes a picture of your Snapcode, so as customers are getting manis or pedis, they can also add you on Snapchat. Mention that you also have a custom geofilter, and they'll likely post pics of your nail work on the spot.

Determine the frequency of how often the majority of repeat customers return, and change out your geofilter based on that frequency whether it's once every 2 weeks, 4 weeks, or some other interval.

If you get creative with your geofilters, customers will be excited to see the new design upon each return.

25. CHIROPRACTORS

Clients will oftentimes show up at your establishment in pain until you have adjusted them. Make your adjustment, and as you debrief how they feel afterwards, inform them that you have a custom geofilter for people to share their experience with friends and family. By simply informing them of the existence of your geofilter, many of them will gladly recommend you because they have immediate relief from their pain.

26. CONSTRUCTION LABORERS

As you construct a new building, you can create geofilters for onlookers as well as other construction laborers to document the construction process on a day-by-day basis. It will create more awareness for your building, and potentially get you more work for other projects.

27. <u>FUNDRAISERS</u>

If you have an upcoming fundraiser, creating a geofilter will help you get the word out and create more awareness for your reason or cause.

Even though it's a fundraiser, consider making your geofilter creative and fun so people are excited to take pictures and share them.

If you happen to know someone who is throwing a fundraiser, maybe offer to make a geofilter for them and get it set up on their behalf as your way to contribute to the cause.

28. <u>REALTORS</u>

Realtors can use geofilters during property showings to increase buzz for each listing. Throw a mixer or luncheon for other realtors as a networking event, and set up a geofilter at the event.

If you happen to be invited to someone else's event, set up a geofilter at the event and use your geofilter as an ice-breaker in getting to know other realtors.

Geofilters will easily and quickly set you apart from others in the industry as a creative marketing expert.

Consider setting up a geofilter at your listing right when it's ready to show. Do a video walk-through while using your own geofilter.

Even though it's unlikely that anyone else will use your geofilter during your walk-through, you create a raw unedited video that makes you come across as genuine and trustworthy, while still branding your video in a professional way with your logo.

You can even put the listing address somewhere on the geofilter so people can swing by and see it.

Any use of your geofilters will also increase the likelihood of other friends hiring you in the future since your brand has been seen in their story and has created top-of-mind awareness.

Note: Don't try to list your MLS number on the geofilter. Doing so will likely get you rejected.

29. BOOKSTORE OWNERS

Use geofilters to showcase new releases. When a publisher offers a new book, they have already created marketing and excitement for the book. By creating a geofilter for the same book release, you are fueling excitement for the book as well as sales for the book. Visitors to your store who may not have been interested in that particular book may wind up purchasing it anyways.

One of the best uses for geofilters for bookstore owners is book signings. If you have an author who visits to signs books, create a geofilter with your bookstore name and the author's name at the bottom. This gives customers the chance not only to get a signed, purchased copy of the book, but it also gives them the chance to get a selfie with the author with your branding on it. If they are excited to get a signed copy of the book, they will be even more excited to share that picture with their friends and family.

30. LIBRARIANS

People often come to the library to simply hang out and read. Set up a geofilter at the library and switch it out often. Visitors will look forward to the new geofilters and give them a new reason to come back more often.

31. VETERINARIANS

While pet owners often bring their animals to a vet when they are sick, they are oftentimes excited to pick them up after their treatment, surgery, or procedure.

Consider making a pet-friendly geofilter that focuses on healthy and happy pets, and other pet owners who see your geofilter in their friends' Snapchat stories will be more likely to use your vet clinic in the future.

32. LAWYERS

Call it confidence or guts, but set up a geofilter congratulating your clients at the courthouse on the day of the trial. If you win, start taking pictures with Snapchat with your clients and they will likely use the filter on their own accounts. This will help fuel your firm's identity and associate your brand with winning.

It goes without saying, but of course you would not use the geofilter if you lost your case. You might feel unethical about setting up a geofilter that is only used if you happen to win; however, consider every major sporting event and the fact that winning hats and shirts for both teams are made ahead of time with the hope that they win. If a team loses, their winning apparel never sees the light of day. If a team wins, they're ready to go.

33. DENTISTS

Give your patients a reason to smile! Set up a custom geofilter, and your patients will likely take more selfies at your practice than any other time.

Don't create a boring and lame geofilter though. Make it fun and exciting so people will naturally want to use it. You can still put your logo on it, but if you can get your patients to smile naturally on their own, you've got a winning opportunity that will make your practice shine.

34. WAITERS / WAITRESSES

Get permission from your manager to set up your own Snapchat geofilter, and you've got an instant ice-breaker any time you see one of your customers using their smart phone.

You can ask, "Are you by chance using Snapchat?" This will lead into a conversation about Snapchat and whether they have it. If they do, you can casually say something like, "Check out my filter" and then walk away. Your customers will be so intrigued that they'll likely go check it out. They'll likely be so impressed that they'll probably take a picture with you in it. The more interaction you have with your customers, the more genuine you can be, and the more relatable you are, the greater experience they will have.

Not only will this get you recognized by your boss and the owner for being cutting-edge, but you will gain the reputation for going the extra mile.

Your customers may begin to start coming back, and if you set up a new and unique geofilter frequently enough, you may start to have many more customers requesting to sit in your section because you simply provide another level of fun and interaction.

Of course serving people should not be all about the money, but your geofilter will likely pay for itself based on the higher tips you will inevitably receive.

35. AUTHORS

Set up a geofilter at your next book signing and offer to

take pictures with fans as they approach your table. They will likely be excited for the opportunity and impressed with your tech savvy.

This will increase the awareness for your book and get your name as an author in front of more people. These new people, however, are likely similar minded to the person who is using your geofilter, so you may generate many new fans and readers as a result.

36. POLITICIANS

Hillary Clinton was the first Democratic Presidential nominee to use Snapchat geofilters leading up to the 2016 election.

Whether you like her or hate her, her campaign was cutting edge for politicians. Not only did she create a geofilter on the last night of the Republican National Convention just to mess with the republicans, but she also offered a national geofilter on the day of the election itself.

There were likely millions of people who saw at least one of her political geofilters, and it marked the beginning of a new era with political ads.

Clinton just barely scratched the surface of what she could do with geofilters as well.

Politicians can and should set up geofilters for every rally, every press release, every campaign stop, and every speech they give. They're too easy and inexpensive not to.

If you are a campaign manager for a politician or you're a politician setting up your own campaign, consider making your geofilters fan-friendly. In other words, focus on the positive side of the campaign and leave any negativity to someone else. Geofilters like "I'm with _____!" will be easy for fans to share rather than feeling guilty about bashing someone else.

37. FUNERAL DIRECTORS

This may be the one exception to the fun rule. While you can still create a geofilter that can be shared at your funeral home, you likely don't want to make it joyous. While those who have lost loved ones may choose to have a celebration of life, you don't want to assume that everyone does.

That being said, this can be a conversation with each family. Maybe offer a free custom geofilter to each family who comes to your establishment as a way to honor the deceased.

It may be helpful to print a few examples of geofilter designs you have already created from which they can pick.

Who knows… maybe some of them will want a happy and joyous filter after all.

38. NON-PROFITS

Set up a geofilter for each event you host. Visitors will gladly share your brand when it's an organization they're proud to support.

This works for all types of non-profits and not-for-profits alike, such as churches, missions organizations, food pantries, etc.

HOW TO INCENTIVIZE YOUR GEOFILTERS

You can motivate Snapchat users to use and share your geofilters by offering them incentives to do so.

Consider offering an immediate discount at the register if they show you on their mobile device that they have shared a photo or video with your filter on their story.

Or maybe consider offering a transferrable coupon for 15% off if they share your geofilter.

Consider combining both concepts by creating a geofilter that shows your incentive of 15% in the actual geofilter itself. The discount can be redeemable on the spot for users who found it, but it can also be redeemable for others who saw it on Snapchat and came in just because they saw it.

Remember that while you cannot include a phone number, hashtag or domain name in your geofilter artwork, you CAN include your physical address.

Regardless of the incentive you offer, the benefits of the advertising you will gain likely far outweighs the cost of whatever the coupon is that you have offered.

SAMPLE GEOFILTERS

In case you have no clue as to what a Snapchat geofilter looks like, the following pages show samples of geofilter designs. Notice that the background image does not change in each sample. This is to help you see the differences in geofilters rather focusing on the image beneath the geofilter.

When using an actual geofilter, users will take their own pictures and then overlay a geofilter on top.

When you design a geofilter, you cannot control what photo or video people will use with your geofilter; you simply control what the design of your geofilter looks like and where geographically it is available for people to use.

While you are limited with what you can include on a geofilter, your design can create buzz, excitement and branding for your event or organization.

Check out the following pages for sample designs. While the interior of this book has been printed in black and white, your geofilters can of course be created in vibrant color.

HOUSE PARTY

HAPPY
BIRTHDAY

HOMECOMING MEMORIES

BFFS
JAN 19, 2017

HOW TO TAKE PICS & VIDS IN SNAPCHAT ▶

Open the app and go to the camera screen.

To take a picture, tap the shutter button on the bottom of the screen within the native camera. You get to select how long you want your picture to be able to viewed by others before it disappears.

To take a video, hold down the shutter button on the bottom of the screen. You can record short videos within Snapchat, but you cannot record long videos.

Scan to view a video tutorial on this chapter, or go to:
http://mattmizell.com/how-to-take-pics-and-vids-in-snapchat

HOW TO USE FILTERS IN SNAPCHAT ▶

Once you have taken a picture or video, hold down on the screen and swipe left. This will bring up one filter among a variety of color-enhancing filters as well as any geofilters that might be available.

Continue swiping left until you find a filter you like. Then release the finger you were holding on the screen and the filter will apply to your photo or video.

Once you have selected a filter, you may add more than one filter using the same process.

Scan to view a video tutorial on this chapter, or go to:
http://mattmizell.com/how-to-use-filters-in-snapchat

HOW TO DESIGN A GEOFILTER WITH PHOTOSHOP ▶

Open Photoshop. Create a new image with transparent background with dimensions of 1080x1920 pixels.

Design whatever you like, ensuring that not "too much" of the screen is covered. (This instruction comes from Snapchat's own rules, but they do not define what "too much" of the screen is. I have had filters rejected because too much of the screen was covered, and it seemed as though it was about 30% of coverage.)

Once you have finished creating your design, save it as a PNG file to preserve the transparent background.

Scan to view a video tutorial on this chapter, or go to:
http://mattmizell.com/how-to-design-a-geofilter-with-photoshop

HOW TO DESIGN A GEOFILTER WITHOUT PHOTOSHOP ▶

There are a ton of free photo editing programs you can use to create filters with transparent backgrounds.

However, you can now use Snapchat's own filter designer directly on their website.

Go to www.snapchat.com > Geofilters > On Demand > Create Filter. If you haven't created a profile yet, you can create one for free.

On the Create Filter page, you can use your own design or create one online. Select the Create Online option and play around with the design tools to create a customized geofilter without using Photoshop.

Scan to view a video tutorial on this chapter, or go to:
http://mattmizell.com/how-to-design-a-geofilter-without-photoshop

WHAT TO DO IF YOUR "ASSET IS TOO LARGE" ►

If you attempt to submit a geofilter design and the site won't allow you to purchase it or you see an error message saying that your "asset is too large", don't take it personally.

Snapchat isn't trying to offend you. They're simply telling you that your image design is too large.

First check to make sure that the dimensions of your image are correct at 1080x1920 pixels.

If the image is the correct size, then the problem is likely that your file size is too big. PNG images cannot be larger than 300kb, so you will have to reduce the file size and upload it again.

To optimize your geofilter by reducing the file size, go to www.tinypng.com and upload your image for free. You can then download it again with a reduced file size. If it is still too large, you can upload the smaller file to www.tinypng.com again and keep reducing the file size until it is under 300kb.

I have personally ran images through www.tinypng.com over a dozen times each and the quality is not noticeably less, and I have successfully reduced the much larger file to under 300kb.

Once you get your file size under 300kb, upload it at www.snapchat.com again and you likely will not encounter the error message any longer.

Scan to view a video tutorial on this chapter, or go to:
http://mattmizell.com/how-to-optimize-your-geofilter

HOW TO SET UP A GEOFILTER CAMPAIGN ▶

Go to www.snapchat.com > Geofilters > On Demand > Create Filter.

If you used Photoshop or another photo editing software to create your design, click the "Use Your Own" link.

If you want to create a design using Snapchat's online designer, click "Create Online".

Once your design has been uploaded or created online, name your design anything you want. (Note: Don't worry about what you name your design. The name won't be visible to anyone in the public. The name is only useful for you to know which advertising campaign it was.) Once you have named your geofilter, click "Next".

Now select when you want your geofilter to show up. Select the date, start time, and ending time for when you want it to be visible. (Note: You can adjust this time on a later page if needed.)

Because Snapchat requires approval of every design, you must submit your design at least 9 hours ahead of your event. Once you have selected your date and times, click "Next".

Now select the actual geofence where your geofilter will show up. (For additional help on how to set up the geofence, read the following chapter entitled *How to Set Up a Geofilter's Geofence.*)

Once you have created your geofence, click "Next". Now you will see your Order Summary and Geofilter Details and payment options.

Double-check all the details to ensure they are correct, enter your credit card information, accept the Terms and Conditions and click "Submit".

If you see an error message saying that your asset is too large, read the previous chapter entitled *What to Do if Your Asset is Too Large.*

Hopefully you will see a confirmation page that says your geofilter has been sent to review.

Your credit card will not be charged until after your design has been reviewed and approved.

You may still cancel your geofilter at any time up until when it is scheduled to go live. If your credit card has already been charged and you choose to cancel your geofilter for whatever reason, Snapchat will give you a full refund. Once your geofilter begins, you can no longer cancel it nor get a refund.

Scan to view a video tutorial on this chapter, or go to:
http://mattmizell.com/how-to-set-up-a-geofilter-campaign

HOW TO SET UP A GEOFENCE ▶

Once you have uploaded your geofilter design at www.snapchat.com, you will have the opportunity to create a geofence that uses GPS to determine where your geofilter will be placed.

First you must upload or create your design at www.snapchat.com. Then select the dates and times for your campaign. Then you will be directed to a page with a map. You can toggle between a map or satellite view when selecting your geofence.

You may type in an address in the search bar if you know the physical address where your event will take place. You may also use the map to navigate to the location of your event. Double-click the screen to zoom in if needed.

When you are ready to select the map coordinates for your geofilter, click "Draw Fence". Your mouse pointer should now be a crosshair.

Click the screen to set a point on the map. Move your cursor to select another point on the map.

Set as many points as you wish, creating a triangle, circle, square, or any shape you like.

Once you are finished with your map layout, click the first point on the map where you started, and your geofence will be set.

The maximum amount of square feet is 5 million, and the minimum amount is 20 thousand square feet. This means that you cannot target an entire city with your geofence. It also means that you cannot target something as small as a single house.

If your advertising campaign requires more than 5 million square feet, you can contact Snapchat directly at www.snap.com to learn about other advertising options.

Scan to view a video tutorial on this chapter, or go to:
http://mattmizell.com/how-to-set-up-a-filters-geofence

WHERE YOU SHOULD BE GETTING CREATIVE ADVICE

If you rely on your own creative instincts for coming up with your geofilter design, you may come up short.

Ask a few people in your target demographic what types of filters they think would connect with other people their same age.

Regardless of the age range of your demographic, get advice from a teenager on what they think would be cool for your geofilter campaign.

Even if your event isn't geared toward teenagers, teens are brilliant marketers and advertisers. Some teens could do a way better job than experienced marketing directors.

The reason why is because teenagers are trained every day on what connects and what doesn't.

They likely haven't gone through college level courses on best marketing practices, but they essentially have a master's degree in what gets likes and what doesn't.

Depending on what teenager you ask, you might get some incredibly lame ideas, but you will likely get some amazing ideas as well.

I *always* get feedback from students for every event that I put on, and while some ideas aren't worth even writing down, I write them down anyways.

A freshman girl recently had "the best idea ever" and suggested that we cover our entire church campus with mattresses for a kickoff event. Despite my initial thoughts of how impractical and pointless her idea was, I wrote it down anyways.

A few weeks later we were brainstorming game ideas for that event, and a friend suggested crowd surfing.

I liked the idea of crowd surfing, but didn't like the idea of students getting groped by other students.

The idea popped into my mind, "Let's use the mattresses!"

We found a few inflatable mattresses, put students on top of them, let them loose in a crowd surfing battle, and it turned out to be one of the best games we've ever done!

Ask for creative advice from your target demographic and you'll be off to a good start.

HOW TO ENSURE YOUR GEOFILTER ISN'T LAME

To ensure your geofilter isn't lame, make sure it doesn't come across business-like. In other words, don't make your geofilter stale and boring.

Think of fun, creative and out-of-the-box ideas for what someone might actually be excited to share with others.

Think of props, cool designs, and eye-catching colors.

If your geofilter has the potential to make someone smile—or better yet, laugh—then you might have a winner.

WHY YOUR GEOFILTER SHOULD BE EXCLUSIVE

Bigger is not always better. Any seasoned salesperson will tell you that exclusivity sells. People want what they can't have.

Rather than making your campaign available to the masses, limit who can see it and when.

While you cannot limit psychographics or demographics of who sees your geofilter, you can determine the exact location based on GPS coordinates of where your geofilter will be available.

Unlike other advertising campaigns that try to reach the masses through print, TV, billboards, etc, you are trying to reach the masses via social connections.

If someone feels as though they are unique, they may be more likely to share.

You might even make Limited Edition geofilters for different locations to help further create the exclusive feel since that particular geofilter will never be made available again.

WHY PLANNING AHEAD IS CRITICAL

All geofilters must be approved by a Snap staff member several hours before it is scheduled to go live. While this is an improvement considering geofilters used to take days to get approved, you still don't want to wait until the last minute to create a campaign since it may not get approved in time.

In fact, you might want to play it safe for your first few geofilters and submit your artwork several days before it needs to go live. This will give you an extra cushion of time just in case your geofilter gets rejected and you have to make some edits in order to get approved.

HOW TO AVOID OVERPAYING FOR ADVERTISING ▶

The easiest way to overpay for your geofilter campaign is to select a geofence that is larger than what you need. Be sure to select only the areas where people will be during an event, launch, party, etc.

When you create your geofence, remember that you can set as many points on the map as you want. This means that if you are creating a geofence for a gathering that will be held in one ballroom at a convention center, you can select just the ballroom rather than the entire convention center. The difference in price is likely significant.

Avoid overpaying for advertising by paying close attention to where your geofence should and should not be. Avoid places where people are not likely to use Snapchat, such as parking lots or in unoccupied parts of large buildings.

Scan to view a video tutorial on this chapter, or go to:
http://mattmizell.com/how-to-avoid-overpaying-for-snapchat-advertising

HOW TO SAVE MONEY ON GEOFILTERS

If you own a brick-and-mortar business or are consistently putting on daily events in the same location, you should consider setting up an annual geofilter campaign.

There are 5 main benefits to an annual geofilter campaign:

1) You will save a considerable amount of money verses setting up a new campaign each day.

2) You are able to switch out your geofilter design as often as you like with no additional charges.

3) You have access to your stats as you do with other geofilters as well.

4) You cultivate regular customers and a reason to return on a consistent basis.

5) You lock in Snapchat's current rates for geofilters for an entire year.

While there are several benefits to an annual campaign, there are also 3 considerable drawbacks.

1) If you change your mind, you cannot get your money back since the annual agreement is non-refundable.

2) While the annual geofilter offer does have the potential to save money, it really only saves money if you plan on using a geofilter at your location every day of the week. If you are not open on some days or if you don't have customers at your venue on some days, the annual geofilter may not wind up saving you money after all.

3) The annual plan auto-renews after 12 months, and while that may be considered a benefit to some, if your campaign auto-renews after a year and you no longer use your geofilter campaign, you will be stuck with another annual subscription since Snapchat does not offer refunds.

If you consistently welcome visitors to the same location every day of the week, purchasing an annual geofilter can be a great option.

HOW TO AVOID GETTING REJECTED ▶

There are some surefire ways to get your geofilter rejected. You will get rejected if your artwork contains:

- URLs
- Hashtags
- Phone numbers
- Texting groups
- Personal information
- Pics of real people
- Inappropriate content
- Too much art

All artwork is approved by an actual Snap staff member, so you likely won't get away with anything if you try to sneak something by them.

This includes attempting to include a URL rather than a business name on the checkout page. (Tried it. Got rejected.)

Considering so many traditional marketing methods are not allowed with Snapchat, you have to get creative with the impression your geofilter will make.

Below are some of the most common reasons that geofilters get rejected by Snap employees:

Do NOT include any hashtags.

Do NOT include any websites or URLs.

Your graphics should not cover too much of the area where people would appear in pictures or videos.

Do NOT include any phone numbers.

Texting groups are not allowed.

You will also get rejected if you attempt to place too many geofilters in the same location at the same time. This isn't published on their website anywhere, but if you attempt to publish more than 4 concurrent geofilters, the subsequent geofilters will all get rejected.

If you want to use several geofilters during one event, a way to work around this limitation is to roll your different geofilters sequentially rather than simultaneously.

If your event takes place from 6:00-10:00p, you could have a geofilter go live at from 5:00-6:00p as people arrive, another from 6:00-7:00p, a third from 7:00-8:00p, and so on. This way people's stories can get loaded with many different types of geofilters all from the same event.

Scan to view a video tutorial on this chapter, or go to:
http://mattmizell.com/how-to-avoid-getting-rejected

WHY YOU NEED A NON-TRADITIONAL CALL-TO-ACTION

With a little creative thinking, you can create a geofilter that still causes someone to take action despite the limitations Snapchat places on the type of text you can add to your geofilter.

For example, your geofilter could say something like:

"Show up tonight for a free gift at the park"

"Screenshot this filter and bring with you between 5-7pm"

"Add this filter to your story and you could win a prize"

It's worth mentioning that your call-to-action CAN include a physical address of where your event will take place.

WHY YOU SHOULD BE TESTING DIFFERENT STYLES

Simple designs have consistently worked best for most of my campaigns.

In my experience, the crazier the design, the less likely they get used.

However, try out a few styles and get feedback from your target market and implement their suggestions.

The other way to test different designs is to get designs submitted by people in your target demographic.

One of my most complicated designs was submitted by an 11th grade high school student. While most of my complicated designs do not do well, because word spread that a student created the design, it wound up performing better than dozens of other campaigns.

Don't just test the designs themselves, but test the designers of the designs. Those with a lot of influence in your targeted demographic may get better results than you or your graphic designer ever would.

THE WRONG PLACE TO ADD TEXT

When designing your geofilter, you may be tempted to put an address or other call-to-action at the very bottom of the screen.

Don't.

The bottom of the screen is where controls for the app pop up, so your text likely will not get seen there.

Instead, put any text that you want read (such as an address) at the top of the geofilter instead of the bottom.

Or if you feel you have to put it at the bottom, give about ¼" of extra space to allow for the app controls.

HOW TO BUILD BUZZ LEADING UP TO AN EVENT

Find out a few locations where your target demographic hang out and create geofilters to promote an event you have coming up.

This helps create the pre-event buzz and builds excitement for what's to come by creating pre-event branding.

HOW TO BUILD EXCITEMENT AT AN EVENT

Don't just use geofilters leading up to an event—use them at your event as well.

Using a geofilter at your event likely won't help get more people to show up, unless your event will take place for many hours or days.

However, it can be effective in making others feel like they missed out, and they'll be more likely to show up to the next event you offer.

An event where all your fans are located at once can create lasting brand recognition since your filter may flood people's Snapchat stories all at once.

HOW TO USE STREAKS TO BUILD YOUR BRAND

A "streak" is created when two Snapchat users send each other snaps on the same day for multiple consecutive days.

For each day both users send snaps back and forth, their streak continues, adding to the number of days they have held their streak with one another.

If either user misses a day, the streak is broken and they have to start over with each other to create a new streak.

Streaks are a powerful force within Snapchat because they reward repetitive intentionality. Friends create streaks with many friends and are proud of dozens of days, if not hundreds of days, of continued streaks.

There is such a psychological draw for students to continue a streak because they don't want to be the one responsible for ruining the fun for the other person who also enjoys having a streak.

What this means for your brand is that you can create streaks with users, and they are likely already trained to keep them up.

How do you create a streak?

Simply send users a private snap, and if they snap you back, you've just created a streak. After they have sent you a return snap, the ball is now in your court to send them a snap the following day.

Once you have created a streak of one day, you will both be notified with an icon within the app next to the other person's username that you have started a streak.

The difficulty is that you actually have to maintain your streaks in order to keep them going. However, if you (or someone you delegate this to) actually takes the time to keep up a streak, you have built in a daily interaction with those users, who will naturally become ravings fans of your brand as a result.

HOW TO USE MULTIPLE GEOFILTERS SIMULTANEOUSLY ▶

Your influencers will likely give you several great ideas. Why not use several of them?

Providing multiple options with different types of geofilters at the same time will make your event look like a really big deal.

As mentioned earlier, Snapchat only allows 4 geofilters to be used by the same account for the same location at the same time. However, geofilters can be purchased in time increments as low as one hour long. This means that you can use up to 4 geofilters per hour.

Using that many geofilters may be overkill unless you have a massive event. However, using a few throughout your event couldn't hurt.

Scan to view a video tutorial on this chapter, or go to:
http://mattmizell.com/how-to-use-multiple-geofilters-at-the-same-time

HOW TO DESIGN GEOFILTER PUZZLES

Snap allows users to apply up to 3 filters at a time to the same picture or video.

Typically users will apply a geofilter featuring a location logo along with a lighting filter. However, you can add whatever filters you want to the same pic or vid.

This means that you can create one geofilter with half of a design and a second geofilter with the other half of the design—like two puzzle pieces fitting together.

Most users won't even catch onto the fact that the layers can overlap each other, but those who *do* figure it out will likely spread your geofilter puzzle they have discovered with many others since the idea is so unique.

As an example, one puzzle geofilter I created featured a set of turntables in a geofilter so students could take a selfie as a DJ. Then in a second geofilter I overlayed a pair of headphones that a student could place over their head while DJing.

Many students used either the turntables *or* the headphones, but the few who figured out they could overlay both geofilters on the same pictures at the same were giddy with excitement, and it created a LOT of discussion.

That is good! If your geofilters are creating discussion, that is a good thing!

HOW TO CREATE GEOFILTER BATTLES

A geofilter battle consists of two or more geofilters, each placed at a different location. The battle encourages users at one location to use their custom filter more than the users at the other location.

For example, target a high school during lunch using one geofilter, and target several other high schools on the same day during their lunches with different geofilters.

Tell students from each school ahead of time to be on the lookout, and let them know they are competing against the other schools to see which school gets the most shares out of their geofilter.

Your battle doesn't have to consist of schools, but you could battle teams, individual employees, departments, churches, neighborhoods, companies, etc.

A twist on the battle idea is to host a scavenger hunt between teams that each use the same geofilter to take pictures of items they find as they find them. A moderator could keep track of which teams find the most items the fastest to determine a winning team.

CELEBRATING SPECIAL EVENTS WITH GEOFILTERS

Geofilters can be used to celebrate someone's birthday, wedding, or other special occasion.

If you are celebrating someone in your organization, co-brand the special event geofilter with the birthday person's name as well as your organization's name. This ensures that whoever sees the special geofilter also sees that your organization is celebrating them. It's a win-win as you make the birthday person feel special and honored while you communicate to their network that your organization cares about its people.

Once the special geofilter is live, tell friends of the celebrating person to use it as many times as possible.

Then after the special geofilter has ended, check the stats a few days later to see how many times their filter was shared and how many people it reached. Then let the celebrated person know the stats from their special geofilter. When they realize that 4,000 people, for example, saw their geofilter, they will likely feel even more special.

HOW AND WHY YOU SHOULD CREATE A SNEAK PREVIEW

Whatever age range you are targeting with your event or brand, recruit a few influencers who are in that same age range.

If you are promoting an event to high schoolers, the last thing you want to do is get a bunch of 30-year-olds using your geofilter.

In the same way, if you are promoting an event to 30-year-olds, the last thing you want are a bunch of teenagers using your geofilter.

To help get the right demographic on board, recruit a few influential people who are in your target demographic and let them know you are creating a geofilter. Tell them exactly where it will be and when it will be there.

Send them a picture of your geofilter ahead of time so they know exactly what it looks like once it goes live.

Ask them to use your geofilter once it goes live so it creates a spark within the correct demographic.

Birds of a feather flock together, right?

Once a spark has been lit by the right influencers, the friends they have influence over may wind up seeing the filter, which helps build the buzz and brand recognition for your event or promotion. There's also a chance they, too, will want to share your filter.

Line up a few influential people in your target demographic and let them in on your cool geofilter coming out.

HOW TO TAKE THE "GEO" OUT OF THE FILTER

It's possible to use geofilters without being at a specific location.

Why would you do this?

Let's say that you're a professional photographer and you want the chance to share some wedding pictures with a Snapchat geofilter featuring your logo, but you prefer to edit your pictures before the world sees them. You may not have time at the wedding itself to download, edit, and upload pictures in time to use a geofilter that is available at the wedding location.

Rather than stress out about getting your pictures edited in too short a time and utilizing a geofilter at the wedding itself, instead create a geofilter with the couple's name and your company logo and set it up to go live at your studio, home, or wherever you edit your photos.

Then after you shoot the wedding on location, head back to your studio, download the pics to your computer, edit them, upload them to your mobile device equipped with

Snapchat, and use your custom geofilter with your logo on the pictures you share.

People who see your pictures on your Snapchat story will presume that you used a geofilter at the wedding itself because all the images were from the wedding.

Not only would your customer be grateful to see the pictures, but you also create brand awareness for others who may be interested in your photography services.

Nobody will know that there wasn't a geofilter at the wedding, but your branding will still be impactful in helping create the story of the wedding.

If you want to really take advantage of this feature, set up two geofilters: one for the wedding itself, and another identical geofilter for your studio. This allows people to use your geofilter at the wedding itself, and then when you upload your images at a later time from a different location, people presume that you somehow magically uploaded all those perfect pictures from the wedding itself since that's where they saw the same geofilter.

Another time this would be helpful is if you happen to forget to create a geofilter for an event. You could still take pictures and videos from your mobile device, and then once you get home create a geofilter from your home and upload the pics and vids with your geofilter.

Of course, using this method does not allow anyone else to use your geofilter, but it does still get your branding and exclusive geofilter into the Snapchat world.

HOW TO SEND PERSONAL MESSAGES IN BULK

The iPhone limits the number of people you can text at the same time, but Snapchat doesn't.

While Snapchat limits the number of people in a group Snap to 16 people, you also have the unique ability to send out a mass snap to as many friends as you like.

This means you can create a custom video invitation or promo and send it to whatever Snapchatters you want within just seconds.

You can use this tool to personally invite people to check out your geofilter once it's live.

Of course they will have to go to the actual physical location where your geofilter is available, but that's kind of the point, right?

HOW TO BEST UTILIZE VIDEOS IN SNAPCHAT ▶

When you are reaching out to your target demographic through personal messages on Snapchat, consider using videos rather than pictures.

You cannot use a video *as* your geofilter design, but you can use a video to *promote* your geofilter design.

Your videos don't have to be professionally made, but they are incredibly useful for engaging individuals within your audience.

Snapchat previously only allowed videos that were shot from within the app itself, but just recently they began allowing users to import pictures or videos from outside the app.

This means that you no longer have to create a video from within the app. You can shoot your footage and then edit your video using iMovie, Final Cut, Premiere, or just your phone, and then upload it to your Snapchat account.

This feature is not widely known, so stories are not yet flooded with great videos, which allows your videos to truly stand out.

Snapchat's new Spectacles are sure to make the usage of video even more prominent within the app.

Scan to view a video tutorial on this chapter, or go to:

http://mattmizell.com/how-to-utilize-high-quality-videos

WHY YOU SHOULD BE USING SPECTACLES ▶

When Snap changed their name from Snapchat, they emphasized part of the reason why is because they are a camera company.

This was evident when they announced the launch of their new video recording glasses known as Spectacles.

Spectacles are unique when it comes to video recording devices, because they record a circle of video rather than a rectangle.

This allows the simultaneous recording of both portrait and landscape video, allowing a user to play back a video recorded as a circle in either portrait or landscape without the screen having to adjust to the orientation of the device.

This feature is currently not available in any other platform, but will presumably become the new norm for video recording devices.

By jumping on board early with new video technology,

your videos will generate discussion and envy all on their own.

To further their exclusivity, Snap made the choice to initially release Spectacles exclusively through Snapbots—vending machines that sold nothing other than Spectacles. Snapbots didn't stay in the same location for long, so people had a limited amount of time to purchase a pair before they disappeared.

In early 2017, Snap began selling Spectacles at www.spectacles.com to the general public, removing the need for tracking down a Snapbot in order to purchase them.

For more information on where and how to purchase Spectacles, visit www.spectacles.com.

Scan to view a video tutorial on this chapter, or go to:
http://mattmizell.com/why-snaps-spectacles-are-a-big-deal

HOW TO CHECK YOUR STATS ▶

Snapchat doesn't provide a lot of demographic information to determine your geofilter's effectiveness. However, they do give you 3 important statistics after a geofilter has been "flighted" or used.

- *Impressions*: the number of people who swiped by your geofilter within the app and saw it as an option as they scrolled through their filter possibilities
- *Conversions*: the number of people who actually used your geofilter while it was live
- *Views*: the number of people who saw your geofilter on someone else's story or sent as a personal snap

All 3 numbers are important, and while Snap may eventually provide more feedback on demographics, the 3 numbers you do currently have access to provide a lot of insight on how effective a campaign really was.

To check the stats for one of your campaigns, log into your account at www.snapchat.com, hover over your profile name in the upper right-hand side of the screen, click on "My Geofilters", and click on any completed campaign.

You should be able to view all 3 of the main statistics from this page for each geofilter campaign you have ever created and launched.

Scan to view a video tutorial on this chapter, or go to:

http://mattmizell.com/how-to-check-your-geofilters-statistics

HOW TO USE YOUR STATS

Don't just read your stats—use them.

Try to determine why a geofilter worked whereas another did not. Was the timing off? Was the design not cool enough? Was it too busy? Was it too lame?

Look at your most impactful campaigns and try to recreate what worked well in other campaigns.

Compare the number of swipes to the number of uses. The number of uses will inevitably be a smaller number than the number of swipes, but what is the percentage?

Do 50% of the people who swipe by your geofilter actually use it? Do 25% of the people who see it use it? Maybe 90%? Learn what is connecting with your audience by comparing swipes to uses.

The number of views tells you your campaign's overall reach. The more uses of your geofilter, the more views you will receive. While the number of views gives you an idea of how many people saw your campaign, most of your energy should be spent on determining how to increase the number of uses for each geofilter.

WHY YOU SHOULD LIMIT YOUR USE OF GEOFILTERS

Once you have launched your campaign and seen some results, you may be tempted to use geofilters all the time.

Resist the temptation.

If you use geofilters for anything and everything, they will lose their exclusive and exciting feel.

Limit when and how you use them, and bring them out for your most-important campaigns so they don't become white noise.

HOW TO POSITION YOURSELF AS A SNAPCHAT GURU ▶

There are two main ways of positioning yourself as a Snapchat expert:

1) **Use On-Demand Geofilters.**

   When others begin to realize that you somehow have inner working knowledge of how to get Snapchat geofilters, they'll realize that you know a thing or two about Snapchat.

2) **Create Community Geofilters.**

   Many of the filters you see at landmarks and cities have been created by individuals who simply submitted them to Snapchat for approval. You can't include any sort of branding for community geofilters, but when others realize that you created a geofilter that is visible to millions, they will consider you to be a Snapchat guru. Rightfully so.

Scan to view a video tutorial on this chapter, or go to:

http://mattmizell.com/how-to-position-yourself-as-a-snapchat-guru

VIDEO TUTORIAL LINKS ►

How to Navigate the Snapchat App

http://mattmizell.com/how-to-navigate-the-snapchat-app

How to Use Filters in Snapchat

http://mattmizell.com/how-to-use-filters-in-snapchat

How to Design A Geofilter with Photoshop

http://mattmizell.com/how-to-design-a-geofilter-with-photoshop

How to Design A Geofilter without Photoshop

http://mattmizell.com/how-to-design-a-geofilter-without-photoshop

How to Use Multiple Geofilters at the Same Time

http://mattmizell.com/how-to-use-multiple-geofilters-at-the-same-time

How to Avoid Over-Paying for Snapchat Advertising

http://mattmizell.com/how-to-avoid-overpaying-for-snapchat-advertising

How to Set Up A Geofilter Campaign

http://mattmizell.com/how-to-set-up-a-geofilter-campaign

How to Avoid Getting Rejected

http://mattmizell.com/how-to-avoid-getting-rejected

How to Set Up A Filter's Geofence

http://mattmizell.com/how-to-set-up-a-filters-geofence

How to Check Your Geofilter's Statistics

http://mattmizell.com/how-to-check-your-geofilters-statistics

How to Optimize Your Geofilter

http://mattmizell.com/how-to-optimize-your-geofilter

How to Take Pics & Vids in Snapchat

http://mattmizell.com/how-to-take-pics-and-vids-in-snapchat

How to Utilize High-Quality Videos

http://mattmizell.com/how-to-utilize-high-quality-videos

How to Position Yourself As A Snapchat Expert

http://mattmizell.com/how-to-position-yourself-as-a-snapchat-guru

Why Snap's New Spectacles Are A Big Deal

http://mattmizell.com/why-snaps-spectacles-are-a-big-deal

ACKNOWLEDGEMENTS

A special thanks to each person who contributed thoughts, perspective, ideas, critique, and promotion to make this book better and possible, including:

Ashten Mizell

Mindy Mizell Galey

Meg Wallace

Daniel Goulding

Kelly Helvie

Keenan Klamer

Nicholas Marsden

Felipe Mendoza

Andrew Riojas

Scott Thetford

Sam White

NOTES

Page 16: Snapchat's renaming to Snap, Inc.

https://www.snap.com/en-US/news

September 24, 2016 blog entry

Pages 18-19: Snapchat statistics

https://www.snapchat.com/ads

Accessed March 31, 2017

Page 30: Snap Ads Max Reach & Goal-Based Bidding

Snapchat unlocked special edition

Accessed March 29, 2017

Page 32: "Tiny pieces of art" quote

https://www.snapchat.com/ads/sponsored-geofilters

Accessed March 29, 2017

Page 122: Snapbots info

https://support.spectacles.com/en-US/article/about-snapbot

Accessed January 28, 2017

ABOUT THE AUTHOR

While sitting in a group brainstorm session, someone threw out the idea of how cool it would be if we could get a custom Snapchat geofilter.

This was shortly after geofilters were launched by Snapchat, so nobody was really thinking about the possibility of creating a custom geofilter.

Matt went to work trying to find out how to convince Snapchat to let him design a geofilter, and as it turned out, Snapchat had just created the opportunity for the general public to purchase geofilters just a few days earlier.

Therefore, Matt launched his first geofilter and blew the minds of students who saw it on their phones a few days later.

Matt has worked with youth for nearly two decades. He leans on them for creative advice and consulting, and in exchange he teaches them how to build legacies based on becoming leaders who are worth following.

Get to know Matt at www.mattmizell.com.

SHARE YOUR THOUGHTS

I would love to know your thoughts on this book.

How can it be improved?

What stood out to you most?

What is missing?

What has changed within Snapchat that should be changed in this book?

What has been most helpful to you from this guide?

Good or bad, feel free to share your opinion by visiting www.mattmizell.com/snapchat-book-review.

SPREAD THE LOVE

If this book has been useful to you in any way, would you consider sharing it with someone else? There are three main ways you can share this content with someone else:

1) **Give someone a physical copy of this book.**
   Maybe you have a friend or family member who works in one of the careers mentioned within this book, and you know the content would be helpful to them. Consider giving them your copy, or better yet, get them a copy of their own.

2) **Send them the link to get this book for free.**
   If you know someone who would benefit from the concepts written in this book, encourage them to download it for themselves for free at www.mattmizell.com/free-snapchat-book.

3) **Share an honest review on Amazon.com.**
   One of the best ways to help others with this book is by helping them find it. By writing a brief review on Amazon.com, you help increase this book's ability to be found by others. You are even able to submit a review if

you did not purchase or acquire the book from Amazon.com. To write a review, visit www.mattmizell.com/snapchat-book-review.

Add me as a friend on Snapchat using the Snapcode above! To do so, take a picture of this page with your mobile device. Then open the Snapchat app, and from the camera screen, swipe down, tap Add Friends, tap Snapcode, select the image of this page, and Snapchat will find my profile for you to add.

I look forward to meeting you!
– Matt Mizell

Download a FREE copy of Matt's ebook,

The Secret to Success

3 Steps to Unlocking Your True Potential,

by visiting www.mattmizell.com/success.

Learn how to build your leadership platform
as a leader worth following by joining the
movement at www.mattmizell.com.

#leaderworthfollowing

Get one of the hottest interactive games
available to build community and fun paranoia.
Visit www.mattmizell.com/blacklist